MINERALS

EARLY BIRD
EARTH SCIENCE

BY SALLY M. WALKER

LERNER PUBLICATIONS COMPANY • MINNEAPOLIS

Text copyright © 2007 by Sally M. Walker

Lerner Publications Company
A division of Lerner Publishing Group
241 First Avenue North
Minneapolis, MN 55401 U.S.A.

Website address: www.lernerbooks.com

Library of Congress Cataloging-in-Publication Data

Walker, Sally M.
    Minerals / by Sally M. Walker.
        p.   cm. — (Early bird earth science)
    Includes index.
    ISBN-13: 978-0-8225-5946-7 (lib. bdg. : alk. paper)
    ISBN-10: 0-8225-5946-3 (lib. bdg. : alk. paper)
    1. Minerals—Juvenile literature. 2. Mineralogy—Juvenile literature. I. Title. II. Series.
QE365.2.W35 2007
549—dc22   2005024010

Manufactured in the United States of America
1 2 3 4 5 6 – JR – 12 10 09 08 07

CONTENTS

BE A WORD DETECTIVE

Can you find these words as you read about minerals?
Be a detective and try to figure out what they mean.
You can turn to the glossary on page 46 for help.

atoms

bond

cement

crystals

igneous rocks

magma

metamorphic rocks

minerals

sedimentary rock

sediments

streak plate

We use minerals (MIHN-ur-uhlz) to write. How else do we use minerals?

CHAPTER 1

WHAT IS A MINERAL?

Minerals are amazing. We use them to build houses. We use them to make jewelry. We even write with a mineral. But what is a mineral?

A mineral is a substance found in nature. Minerals are solid. They are not alive, like plants and animals are. Earth has more than 3,500 different kinds of minerals.

This mineral is called graphite (GRA-fite). Graphite is used in pencils.

Minerals are made of atoms. Everything in the world is made of atoms. Atoms make up trees, clouds, rocks, books, and you. Atoms are very tiny. Billions of atoms could fit on the dot over the letter *i*. There are many different kinds of atoms.

Atoms make up rocks such as these.

Only one kind of atom is in this piece of gold.

Some minerals are made of only one kind of atom. Gold is a mineral made only of gold atoms. Another mineral, called silver, is made only of silver atoms.

This mineral is called calcite (KAL-site). It is made of three kinds of atoms.

Most minerals are made of two or more kinds of atoms. Some atoms pull on one another. When they do, the atoms can bond. Bonding is joining together. A mineral forms when certain atoms bond. Bonding holds the atoms tightly together.

A mineral called halite (HAL-ite) is made from atoms called chlorine (KLOR-een) and sodium (SOH-dee-uhm). Halite is found in many places. Most people call halite by another name. They call it salt!

This is halite. Halite is salt. You might find it on your kitchen table.

Graphite and diamond are minerals. Both graphite and diamond are made only of carbon atoms. But graphite and diamond look nothing alike. Why don't graphite and diamond look alike?

Graphite and diamond don't look alike because their atoms are arranged in different ways. The atoms inside each mineral are packed together in a certain way. Every mineral has its own special arrangement of atoms.

The mineral on the left is graphite. The mineral on the right is diamond.

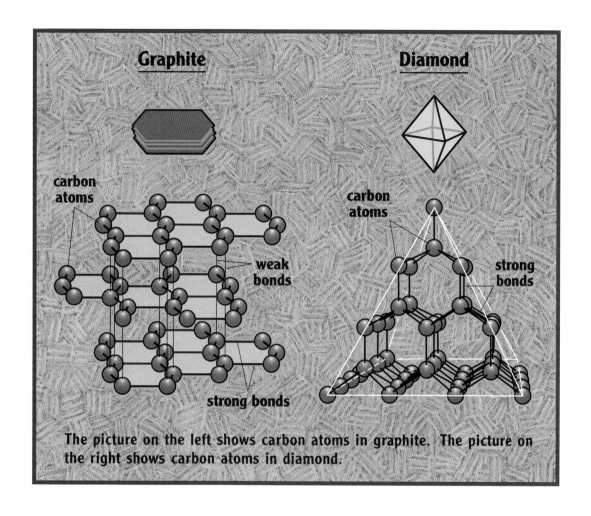

Graphite

Diamond

carbon
atoms

weak
bonds

strong bonds

carbon
atoms

strong
bonds

The picture on the left shows carbon atoms in graphite. The picture on the right shows carbon atoms in diamond.

In graphite, the carbon atoms are arranged in flat sheets. The sheets can break apart easily. This makes graphite soft.

In diamond, the carbon atoms are arranged in a way that makes them stay tightly together. This makes diamond hard.

Minerals make very pretty crystals (KRIHS-tuhlz).

A mineral's atoms can make shapes called crystals. A crystal gets its shape from the way the atoms inside it are arranged. Crystals have smooth, flat surfaces and sharp edges.

Crystals can be many different shapes.
Some crystals are long and have pointed ends.
Others are shaped like cubes.

These crystals have long shapes.

Crystals need room to grow. Crystals can become very big if they have lots of open space to grow. Crystals can grow even bigger than you!

Some crystals are large.

Most crystals do not grow large.

Most crystals stay small. They don't have enough room to grow big. Sometimes many crystals are packed tightly together. The flat surfaces squeeze into one another. You cannot see the different crystals anymore.

This piece of quartz (KWORTZ) looks pink. But quartz is not always pink. Do you know why?

CHAPTER 2
DESCRIBING MINERALS

Minerals come in many different colors. They can be hard or soft. They can be many shapes and sizes. Describing minerals helps us to identify them.

This piece of quartz has a grayish color.

Describing a mineral's color may be easy. But color is not the best way to identify a mineral. A mineral may not always have the same color. Sometimes different atoms get trapped inside a mineral when it forms. These different atoms can change the color of the mineral.

A better way to describe a mineral is by testing its hardness. Some minerals are very soft. One soft mineral is called talc. A person's fingernail can scratch talc.

Talc is a soft mineral.

Diamonds are the hardest mineral. A diamond can scratch glass.

Other minerals are hard. Quartz is much harder than talc. A metal nail is not hard enough to scratch quartz. But a diamond can scratch quartz. Diamond is the hardest mineral of all.

Scientists compare the hardness of different minerals. They use a special scale. This scale gives numbers to minerals. Soft minerals have low numbers. Hard minerals have high numbers. Hard minerals can scratch soft minerals. The higher a mineral's number is, the more minerals it can scratch.

Mohs' Scale

Hardness	Mineral
1	Talcum powder
2	Gypsum
3	Calcite
4	Fluorite
5	Apatite
6	Orthoclase
7	Quartz
8	Topaz
9	Corundum
10	Diamond

Hardness of Other Items

Hardness	Item
2.5	Fingernail
3	Penny
4–5	Iron nail
5.5	Kitchen knife blade

Scientists use a scale for measuring minerals' hardness. It is called Mohs' scale. The chart on the left is Mohs' scale. The chart on the right shows the hardness of some other items.

Streak plates such as this help us to study minerals.

A tool called a streak plate also helps us to study minerals. A streak plate is made of white tile. People scrape minerals across streak plates. Some of the minerals make colored lines on the plates. Different minerals make lines that are different colors. The lines are tiny bits that have scraped off of the minerals. A mineral called hematite (HEE-muh-tite) makes a reddish brown streak. The mineral quartz makes a white streak.

Some minerals break apart in a special way. The broken edges have smooth, flat surfaces. The arrangement of the minerals' atoms make them break this way. Mica (MY-kuh) is a mineral that breaks apart in flat surfaces. A person can pull mica apart into very thin sheets. Mica is easy to identify by the way it breaks.

Mica breaks apart in flat surfaces.

Halite and galena (guh-LEE-nuh) can be identified by the ways they break too. They break smoothly in more than one direction. Their flat, broken edges make pieces shaped like cubes.

Galena breaks smoothly in more than one direction.

The way a mineral's surface looks helps scientists to identify it. Light makes a diamond's flat surfaces sparkle brightly, like glass. Some minerals look like shiny metal.

This mineral is galena. Its surface shines like metal.

This mineral is turquoise (TUR-kwoyz). It has an oily surface.

Some minerals look like they have oil on their surfaces. Other minerals look dull. Their surfaces do not shine.

Minerals can make things.
Do you know what happens
when minerals mix together?

CHAPTER 3

HOW DO MINERALS BECOME ROCKS?

Earth's minerals are very important. When the minerals mix together, they become rocks. Rocks are everywhere on Earth.

Chains of rocky mountains rise above Earth's surface. Melted rocks are deep inside Earth. But how do minerals become rocks?

Rocks are everywhere on Earth.

It is very hot deep inside Earth. It is so hot that rocks melt. Melted rock inside Earth is called magma (MAG-muh). Magma is made of many minerals. As magma cools, the minerals harden together and become rock. Rocks made from cooled magma are called igneous (IHG-nee-uhs) rocks.

These igneous rocks are made from cooled magma.

Granite (GRAN-iht) is an igneous rock. Granite contains the minerals quartz, feldspar, and mica. Gray-colored crystals in granite are quartz. Pink crystals are feldspar. Mica crystals can be black or gray.

Can you see the quartz, feldspar, and mica inside this piece of granite?

Earth has an outer layer called the crust. Earth's crust is very heavy. It presses down on rock that is under it. The pressing can make heat. Heat and squeezing changes rocks. Rocks changed by heat and squeezing are called metamorphic (MEH-tuh-MOR-fihk) rocks.

Heating and squeezing created this metamorphic rock.

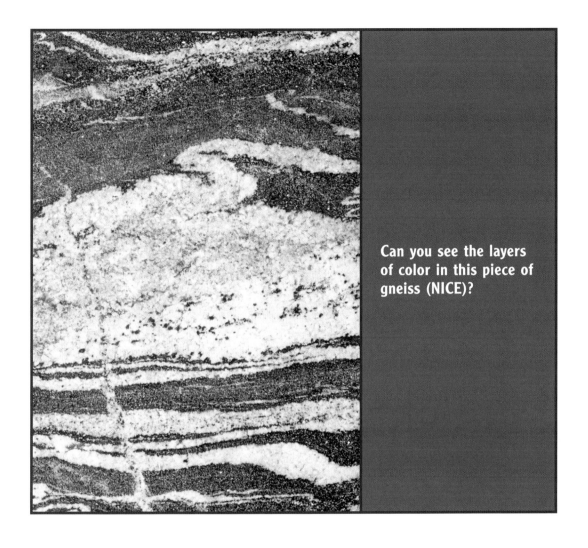

Can you see the layers of color in this piece of gneiss (NICE)?

Gneiss is one kind of metamorphic rock. Gneiss forms when the minerals in a piece of granite are squeezed and heated. The squeezing and heat make the mineral's atoms line up. The atoms become layers of different colors.

Water dissolves some minerals. Water with dissolved minerals in it flows under the ground. The dissolved minerals fill tiny spaces between bits of mud, sand, stone, shell, and bone. Bits of mud, sand, stone, shell, or bone are called sediments (SEH-duh-mehnts). The minerals cement (sih-MEHNT) the sediments together. Cementing is gluing together. The cemented sediments become a kind of rock called sedimentary (SEH-duh-MEHN-tuh-ree) rock.

Cemented sediments make up this sedimentary rock.

Limestone is made of sediments. It is a sedimentary rock.

Limestone is a sedimentary rock. Limestone is formed when water that contains the mineral calcite surrounds sediments. The calcite cements the sediments together. They become limestone.

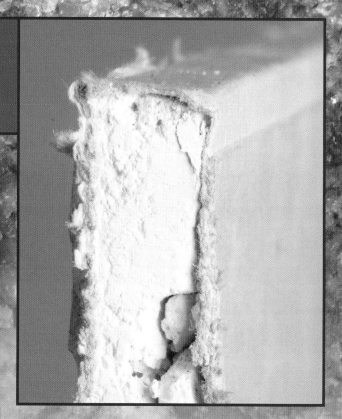

This is a gypsum (JIHP-suhm) sheet. It is made of a mineral called gypsum. Do you know how we use gypsum sheets?

CHAPTER 4

HOW DO PEOPLE USE MINERALS?

People use minerals in many ways. We grind a mineral called gypsum into a powder. The powder is mixed with liquid. Then it is made into flat, solid sheets. The sheets are used as walls in homes and other buildings.

Toothpaste contains a mineral called fluorite (FLUR-ite). Fluorite helps to keep your teeth healthy and clean.

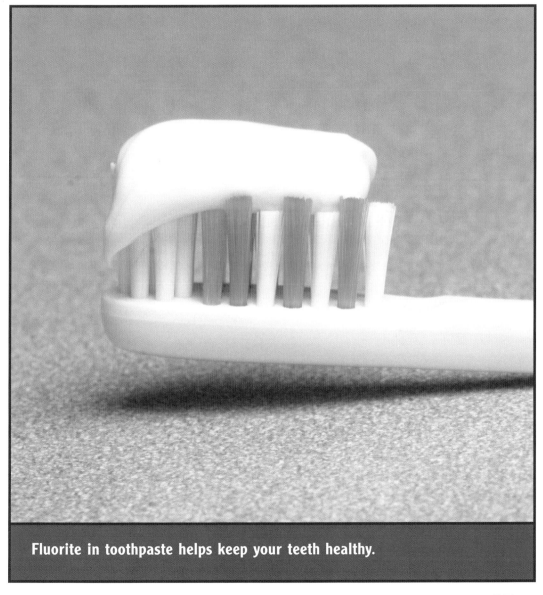

Fluorite in toothpaste helps keep your teeth healthy.

Some minerals can be made into metals. Copper is a metal that is made from a mineral. Some wire is made out of copper. The electricity in our homes, schools, and offices often flows through copper wires.

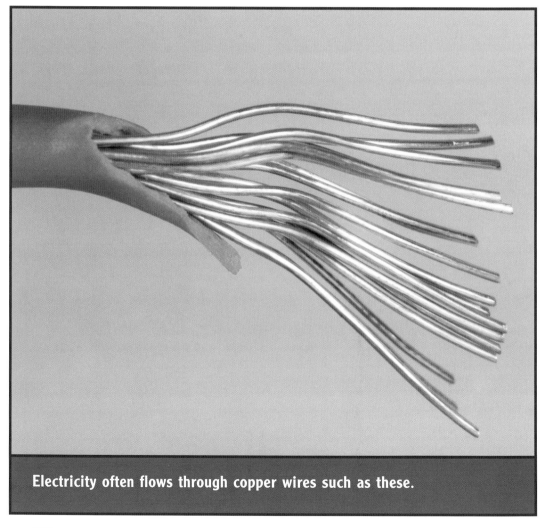

Electricity often flows through copper wires such as these.

This mineral is in your bones and teeth.

Did you know that you have a mineral inside your body? Your bones and teeth are made of a mineral called apatite (AP-uh-tite).

This baseball bat contains the mineral bauxite (BAWKS-ite).

The mineral bauxite is made into a metal called aluminum (ah-LOOM-ihn-uhm). We use aluminum to make the frames of windows and doors. Aluminum baseball bats are made from bauxite too.

The mineral titanium (ty-TAY-nee-uhm) may have helped to decorate your home. Titanium gives a white color to some paints, paper, and plastic materials.

White paint often contains the mineral titanium.

Minerals are an important part of Earth. They are the ingredients needed to make rock. They are useful for making things.

Workers take minerals from places called mines. Then people use the minerals to make things. This is a copper mine.

This is copper ore. Have you ever seen copper ore up close?

Minerals are beautiful to look at. You may be surprised by how many minerals you see every day. What minerals can you find where you live?

ON SHARING A BOOK

When you share a book with a child, you show that reading is important. To get the most out of the experience, read in a comfortable, quiet place. Turn off the television and limit other distractions, such as telephone calls. Be prepared to start slowly. Take turns reading parts of this book. Stop occasionally and discuss what you're reading. Talk about the photographs. If the child begins to lose interest, stop reading. When you pick up the book again, revisit the parts you have already read.

BE A VOCABULARY DETECTIVE

The word list on page 5 contains words that are important in understanding the topic of this book. Be word detectives and search for the words as you read the book together. Talk about what the words mean and how they are used in the sentence. Do any of these words have more than one meaning? You will find the words defined in a glossary on page 46.

WHAT ABOUT QUESTIONS?

Use questions to make sure the child understands the information in this book. Here are some suggestions:

> What did this paragraph tell us? What does this picture show? What do you think we'll learn about next? What is a mineral? How many kinds of minerals are there? What is the best way to describe a mineral? Can you name some different kinds of minerals? How do we use minerals? What is your favorite part of this book? Why?

If the child has questions, don't hesitate to respond with questions of your own, such as What do *you* think? Why? What is it that you don't know? If the child can't remember certain facts, turn to the index.

INTRODUCING THE INDEX

The index helps readers find information without searching through the whole book. Turn to the index on page 48. Choose an entry such as *streak plates,* and ask the child to find out how people use streak plates to study minerals. Repeat with as many entries as you like. Ask the child to point out the differences between an index and a glossary. (The index helps readers find information, while the glossary tells readers what words mean.)

LEARN MORE ABOUT
MINERALS

BOOKS

Blobaum, Cindy. *Geology Rocks!: 50 Hands-on Activities to Explore the Earth.* **Charlotte, VT: Williamson Publishing Co., 1999.** This book about rocks and minerals includes fun activities you can try.

Christian, Peggy. *If You Find a Rock.* **San Diego: Harcourt, 2000.** This book is an introduction to many different kinds of rocks.

Gans, Roma. *Let's Go Rock Collecting.* **New York: HarperCollins, 1997.** Read all about rocks and learn how you can collect them.

Parker, Steve. *Rocks and Minerals.* **New York: DK Publishing, 1997.** Learn more about rocks and minerals in this interesting book.

WEBSITES
Mineral Matters
http://www.sdnhm.org/kids/minerals
This site from the San Diego Natural History Museum talks about how to identify minerals and how to collect minerals and rocks. It also includes activities and games.

Rocks for Kids
http://www.rocksforkids.com
This page talks about how rocks and minerals form, how to identify rocks and minerals, and how rocks and minerals are used.

Science News for Kids
http://www.sciencenewsforkids.org
This site has articles all about science. It also has games, science fair news, and information on science experiments.

GLOSSARY

atoms: tiny particles. Everything in the world is made of atoms.

bond: to join together

cement (sih-MEHNT): to glue together

crystals (KRIHS-tuhlz): minerals that have shapes with flat surfaces and sharp edges

igneous (IHG-nee-uhs) rocks: rocks made from melted minerals

magma (MAG-muh): melted rock inside Earth

metamorphic (MEH-tuh-MOR-fihk) rocks: rocks that have been changed by heat and squeezing

minerals (MIHN-ur-uhlz): substances found in nature. Minerals are solid. They are not alive.

sedimentary (SEH-duh-MEHN-tuh-ree) rock: rock that forms when bits of mud, sand, stone, shell, or bone are glued together

sediments (SEH-duh-mehnts): bits of mud, sand, stone, shell, or bone

streak plate: a tool for studying minerals. People scrape minerals across streak plates to see if the minerals make colored lines.

INDEX

Pages listed in **bold** type refer to photographs.